JAPANESE GAR

The beauty of Japanese gardens is based on a fundamental paradox: complex rules of composition and symbolism have been applied to create an effect of apparent naturalness and simplicity. Often these rules derive from expressions of traditional Shinto or Buddhist beliefs, but other factors are related to the natural characteristics of Japan's landscape and climate, which undergo dramatic seasonal change, or to the social and economic context within which the gardens were created over a period of centuries.

Distinguishing features of Japanese gardens include the presence of rock groupings (perhaps a reflection of prehistoric reverence for natural rock structures), as well as groves of trees and bodies of water that were thought to indicate sacred ground. Early gardens may have been miniaturized versions of rugged seascapes; later Chinese and Korean influence contributed not only Buddhist-related elements, but also stone fountains and bridges of continental Asian origin. At the same time, Chinese and Korean customs of using gardens for court functions made some of them into more formal and ceremonial places.

The subsequent development of Japanese gardens was strongly influenced by Buddhist doctrines, for many of the early garden designers were monks, and many noted gardens part of temple grounds. Some gardens were designed to offer a Buddhist vision of paradise; others, created in the *kare sansui* (or dry mountain stream) style, were waterless and treeless arrangements of rocks and sand related to a minimalist Zen esthetic also evident in ink painting and bonsai. Garden design was also regarded as a part of architecture: residential structures were built with a view of a garden that served as a virtual extension of the small interior. The growth in popularity of the tea ceremony during the rise of the samurai class in the Muromachi period (1333–1568) brought to Japanese gardens the presence of stone basins, pathways, and lanterns, and simple pavilions. In the succeeding Edo Period (1600–1868), combinations of elements and traditions led to the flourishing of the *kaiyu* (or many pleasures) style, in which a variety of images might await a visitor walking alongside a pond or winding stream.

The result of this harmony of influences is that the Japanese garden today is found in several forms: the stroll garden, in which a path leads from one lovely scene to another; the tea garden, conceived to provide a setting for a calm and graceful ceremony in which views may change with the season or the time of day; the contemplation garden, in which a scene viewed from within a structure can, in the balanced composition of its components, offer an unending source of tranquility and spiritual enrichment. Other gardens provide larger-scale areas designed for amusements or spectacles. But all these gardens reflect the common commitment of their creators and those who look after them today to preserving a sense of wonder for and appreciation of the endless variety of nature's beauty.

Notes On The Illustrations

1. Ritsurin Park (Takamatsu City, Kagawa Pref.)
Begun in the mid-seventeenth century by the lords of the Matsudaira clan, this enormous garden took more than a hundred years to complete. It was made into a public park in 1875. The tea house shown is called the Kikugetsu-tei, or Chrysanthemum Moon Pavilion.

2. Tei-En Garden of Taizo-in Temple (Kyoto)
The main hall of this temple was transported from Nijo castle in the late sixteenth century. Its graceful garden incorporates many unusually-shaped mountain stones.

3. Sanbo-in Garden of Daigo-ji Temple (Kyoto)
Completed in 1624, this garden incorporates waterfalls, islands, and numerous bridges of earth, stone, and wood, as well as carefully selected stones and trees.

4. Byodo-in Garden (Uji City, Kyoto Pref.)
The main feature of this garden is the pond that spreads out in front of the Ho-o Hall, built in 1052-53. The image of the Ho-o Hall sparkling on the wavelets when viewed from the opposite shore of the pond is designed to suggest the image of the Treasure Pond described in Buddhist sutras.

5. Rikugi-en Garden (Tokyo)

Built in the early eighteenth century by a favorite of the Shogun Tsunayoshi, on land given to him by his illustrious patron, this lovely stroll garden in the heart of Tokyo offers a tranquil refuge from the city.

6. Katsura Rikyu Garden (Kyoto)

Construction of the Katsura Rikyu palace was begun in the early seventeenth century by an imperial prince. The picture shows the stone bridges over the pond in front of the Shokin-tei teahouse in the palace garden.

7. Isui-en Garden (Nara)

This garden is divided into eastern and western sections, each with its own pond, connected by a narrow stream. The tea house in the eastern garden looks out toward Nara's famed Todai-ji Temple.

8. Garden of the Ginkaku-ji, or Temple of the Silver Pavilion (Kyoto)

Originally built by the Shogun Yoshimasa, this villa and its grounds were converted into a temple after his death in 1490, as specified in his will. The outer walls of the pavilion were originally intended to be covered in silver foil, but this was never done.

9. Kenroku-en Garden (Kanazawa City, Ishikawa Pref.)

This garden was completed in 1837, two hundred years after its conception by the lord of the Kaga Domain, Maeda Toshinaga. Finely crafted stone bridges and lanterns adorn a landscape criss-crossed by paths, streams, and bridges.

10. Iris Garden of the Meiji Shrine (Tokyo)

The land on which the Meiji Shrine now stands became imperial property in 1884. The iris garden was created by imperial order in 1897 on a strip of land 220 meters long and about 7.5 meters wide, which was formerly used for rice cultivation. Every June the garden shimmers with the blooms of more than 1500 flag irises.

11. Daisen-in Garden, Daitoku-ji Temple (Kyoto)

This garden is a masterpiece of the dry mountain stream style, in which rocks are meant to represent streams and waterfalls, evoking Chinese-style landscape ink paintings of the Muromachi Period. The composition succeeds in coveying the impression of vast mountain ranges, roaring waterfalls, swiftly running streams and quiet pools, all within the confines of this hundred-square-meter garden.

12. Omotesenke Fushin-an Uchi-roji (Kyoto)

The Fushin-an was built by Koshin Sosa, grandson of the legendary sixteenth-century tea master Sen no Rikyu. Its "roji" is a small garden intended as a setting remote from everyday life in which to conduct the tea ceremony.

13. Rock Garden of Ryoan-ji Temple (Kyoto)

Thought to date back to the fifteenth century, this famous Zen garden is renowned for its simplicity. It consists of five groups of stones positioned within approximately 250 square meters of raked white gravel.

14. Garden of the Shojuraiko-ji Temple (Otsu City, Shiga Pref.)

This garden, dating from the late sixteenth century, forms an almost perfect square. It is quite uncommon in that its design, inspired by the dry mountain stream style, also incorporates the compositional principles of Japanese flower arrangement.

15. Okayama Koraku-en Garden (Okayama City, Okayama Pref.)

This famous garden, originally the property of the lords of the Ikeda clan, was completed in 1700, and opened to the public in 1871. A walk through the garden provides many views of the winding stream that marks the scenery, typical of stroll gardens of this kind.

16. Zuisen-ji Garden (Kamakura City, Kanagawa Pref.)

This fourteenth-century garden is built around a winding path that traces its way through eighteen turns, from the study at the garden's entrance, across a small pond, and up the steep mountainside to a viewing platform at the summit. The trip is said to symbolize the journey of life: True understanding waits at the end of many travails, just as the view from the mountaintop awaits the climber of this arduous garden path.

17. Bankokuhaku Kinen Koen Memorial Park (Suita City, Osaka Pref.)

This enormous public garden was originally created by the Japanese government for the World Exposition of 1970 in Osaka. A walk along the stream that flows through the park takes the visitor through examples of ancient, medieval, and modern styles of Japanese garden design.

18. Sanzen-in Garden (Kyoto)

A garden of cedar trees and moss-covered earth surrounds the main hall of the temple, known as the Ojogokuraku-in (the Temple of Rebirth in Paradise). The main hall is thought to have been built around 1150.

19.Moss Garden of the Saiho-ji Temple (Kyoto)

The Zen priest Muso (1275-1351) spent his last years laying out the garden in this private temple. The pond, together with the rest of the garden, represents a scene from the Buddhist Western Paradise.

20. Tenju-an Garden of Nanzen-ji Temple (Kyoto)

The eastern garden of Nanzen-ji's Tenju-an retreat (early fourteenth century) is in the dry mountain stream style, with geometrically shaped stones forming a pavement leading up to the main hall and surrounded on either side by large stones and white gravel, accented with green moss.

21. Raikyu-ji Garden (Takahashi City, Okayama Pref.)

This garden is thought to be an early work of Kobori Enshu, a prominent soldier and tea practitioner of the early seventeenth century. The presence of azalea bushes provides an unusual variation on the usual arrangement of rocks and sand typical of the dry mountain stream style.

22. Zuiho-in Garden (Kyoto)

The garden of this Zen temple (founded in the mid-sixteenth century) utilizes dry-gardening techniques to represent a desolate peninsula, buffeted by waves.

23. Genkyu-en Garden (Hikone City, Shiga Pref.)

This large stroll garden, completed around 1680, provides a fine view of Hikone castle. The garden's name is derived from a detached imperial palace of Tang Dynasty China.

24. Garden of the Kinkaku-ji, or Temple of the Golden Pavilion (Kyoto)

The Golden Pavilion was originally built as a villa by the Shogun Yoshimitsu (died 1408), and was converted into a temple after his death. It was destroyed by arson in 1950, but an exact reproduction was completed in 1955. The view of the pavilion from the shore of the lake that surrounds it is meant to represent a scene from the Buddhist Western Paradise.

Ritsurin Park (Takamatsu City, Kagawa Pref.)

Sanbo-in Garden of Daigo-ji Temple (Kyoto)

Byodo-in Garden (Uji City, Kyoto Pref.)

Rikugi-en Garden (Tokyo)

Katsura Rikyu Garden (Kyoto)

Photograph by Sadao Hibi

Isui-en Garden (Nara)

Garden of the Ginkaku-ji, or Temple of the Silver Pavilion (Kyoto)

Kenroku-en Garden (Kanazawa City, Ishikawa Pref.)

Iris Garden of the Meiji Shrine (Tokyo)

Daisen-in Garden, Daitoku-ji Temple (Kyoto)

Omotesenke Fushin-an Uchi-roji (Kyoto)

Garden of the Shojuraiko-ji Temple (Otsu City, Shiga Pref.)

Tei-En Garden of Taizo-in Temple (Kyoto)

Rock Garden of Ryoan-ji Temple (Kyoto)

Photograph by Dandy Photo

Okayama Koraku-en Garden (Okayama City, Okayama Pref.)

Zuisen-ji Garden (Kamakura City, Kanagawa Pref.)

Bankokuhaku Kinen Koen Memorial Park (Suita City, Osaka Pref.)

Sanzen-in Garden (Kyoto)

Moss Garden of the Saiho-ji Temple (Kyoto)

Tenju-an Garden of Nanzen-ji Temple (Kyoto)

Raikyu-ji Garden (Takahashi City, Okayama Pref.)

Zuiho-in Garden (Kyoto)

Genkyu-en Garden (Hikone City, Shiga Pref.)

**Garden of the Kinkaku-ji, or Temple of the Golden
Pavilion (Kyoto)**

Photograph by Syusuke Sibata